Mars Poetica

Mars Poetica

Wyn Cooper

WHITE PINE PRESS / BUFFALO, NEW YORK

White Pine Press
P.O. Box 236 Buffalo, NY 14201
www.whitepine.org

Publication of this book was made possible, in part, by public funds
from the New York State Council on the Arts, a State Agency; with
funds from the National Endowment for the Arts, which believes that a
great nation deserves great art; and the Witter Bynner Foundation for
Poetry.

Cover Photograph: "New Beginnings" by S. J. Edwards. Copyright © 2018
by S. J. Edwards. https://reyadawnbringr.wixsite.com/silveryesterdays

Author photograph © 2018 Sarah Lavigne.

Printed and bound in the United States of America.

Library of Congress Control Number: 2017946295

ISBN 978-1-945680-13-7

For Shawna

If we are interested in Mars at all, it is only because we wonder over our past and worry terribly about our possible future.

— Ray Bradbury

Contents

I

Mars Poetica / 15

The Kind of Rain / 16

This Lightness / 17

Plaza de Toros / 18

Viral / 19

Movement / 20

Lifeboat / 21

This Train / 22

The Next New Thing / 23

Rosemary's Babies / 24

Angels / 25

My Idea / 26

What I Might Have Done / 27

II

How Silent the Trees / 31

Hurricane / 32

Pity / 33

Quake / 34

Pulse / 35

Drummer / 36

Sort it Out / 37

Mixup at the Speakeasy / 38

Her Measured Fall / 39

Gravity / 40

Counting / 41

The Loneliest Road in America / 42

III

Collected Works / 45

Needles and Haste / 46

Vectors / 47

Gunfire / 48

Intense / 49

Death of the Cool / 50

Tread Lightly / 51

Harvest Moon / 52

Trapped in a Decade Long Gone / 53

She Erased His Mouth / 54

Alaska / 55

Pirated / 56

Debris / 57

IV

Abstraction / 61

Drinking the Stars / 62

Menu / 63

Parade / 64

Three Loves / 65

Flow / 66

Belief / 67

The Watcher / 68

Documents / 69

Film / 70

Starboard / 71

The Road Ends Here / 72

Acknowledgments / 73

Thank You / 74

About the Author / 75

I

Mars Poetica

Imagine you're on Mars, looking at earth,
a swirl of colors in the distance.
Tell us what you miss most, or least.

Let your feelings rise to the surface.
Skim that surface with a tiny net.
Now you're getting the hang of it.

Tell your story slantwise,
streetwise, in the disguise
of an astronaut in his suit.

Tell us something we didn't know
before: how words mean things
we didn't know we knew.

The Kind of Rain

that makes you want to direct
a French film, maybe star in it,
cigarette in hand in Marseille,
sidewalks streaming, sirens blaring
a song you've heard before,
soundtrack that makes you spin
toward Aix, toward Cannes,
speaking the language, smiling
at cameras so small you wonder
how you'll fit into their pictures.

This Lightness

It shows tremendous presence
without a lot of weight,
this wine from Côte-Rôtie,

this supermodel from
Vouvray who cheats at poker,
legs better than the wine's,

this lightness in my step
as I step out today
prepared for mystery,

history that happens by
itself, nothing to dampen
my spirit, my syrah,

my reverie.

Plaza de Toros

The latest word from the stable is that the bull you plan to face
wants nothing to do with you. He feels you are below him, that to
slice you with a horn will shame his family. This information was
gleaned from the marks he made in dirt, the quick left, the long
right. If you wish to send him a message you need to get down on
all fours and convince him you're worthy. The sky in Malaga is
grey as his eyes, and threatening. You check your fear in the mirror,
breathe deeply, enter the ring.

Viral

Click click click,
fingers on keyboards,
not piano but computer,
report instead of song—
no chorus or bridge,
just "suggestions
to increase efficiency."

On the grass outside
corporate headquarters,
a destitute man
with a castoff guitar
writes a country song
to replace the one
he's been in too long.

A passerby records it
on her tiny phone
and posts it online—
his song is heard
by a boy in Tehran,
a guard in Korea,
a barmaid in London.

He's famous for minutes
but doesn't know it,
starts gathering bottles
for their deposits,
cigarette butts for what
they have left that he
might use, his muse.

Movement

A murder of crows flies over us,
cows in a field walk in line
instead of side by side, tractor
slowly plows another field.
Cars drive by from time to time,
robins soar from tree to tree
to telephone line, which
sways under their feathery weight,
making local exhanges hazy.
Branches and leaves wave in a wind
that blows circles of dust into the air,
clogs our lungs and makes us cough
until we see clouds coming fast.

We laugh and laugh—the weather's why
we left—then dredge up stories
from the years we lived here, among
cows and plows and pines, before we
settled in a city of other movements,
found rhythms that suit us better,
we tell ourselves over and over.

Lifeboat

We float through marshes
        where grass grows in tufts
                along the watercourse

that tries so hard to sink
        the lifeboat we have made
                from tenacity and rope,

no dock in sight.

This Train

If this train I'm driving
had brakes I wouldn't

use them, but it doesn't,
so I can't, thus my hurried

journey inland, lush
or arid depending on

which loose track I follow,
which river I parallel

on two thin rails, nails
in the coffin of a common life.

What I find there causes me
to slow down, look around,

think of all the things I said
I didn't mean, and those

I did—to be remembered
by a select few, like you,

when I run out of track.

The Next New Thing

Darling of couture,
petri dish of fashion,
tell me which way
the mistral blows today,
toward the cuts of Milan
or the billows of Paris,
the stark New York style
or the bright hues of Rio.

What's in the air for fall,
charity or schadenfreude,
a toned-down boho look?
Please know I'm going
insane with desire
for the next new thing,
style that won't come back.

Rosemary's Babies

Crickets crescendo, birds diminuendo,
night falls as I sit and stare
at clouds about to disappear
into air as thin as Mia Farrow
in *Rosemary's Baby*: New
Yorkers in thrall to the devil
instead of the dollar, city now
taunted and tainted by money, honey
the bees can't ever deliver fast
enough, drones who serve their queen,
who preens on request, leaves bequests
to museums instead of the hungry.

At night I dream again and again
of ankles that tilt in the morning light,
slim women on their way to work
after their own dreams, not of babies
but of dollars, the shoes they will buy
in Soho and the pillaged Village.

Angels

Better get your angel on, said Jennifer, her voice lower and more urgent than the usual laid-back tone I spent two charmed summers listening to, on the grass, at the beach, the world beyond our reach, the clouds a sign that angels might exist—not that we mentioned it, focused instead on the wonder of our survival, light leaking through rotted boards that looked like what we had fled, bad friends, worse habits, the chances we took so different from how I remember those summers: night rides to Hoosick Falls to shoot pool in pairs, the way she combed her hair, the skirts she wore.

My Idea

My idea of a piece of sculpture is a road.

— Carl Andre

My idea of heaven is a road
that winds and winds toward home.

My idea of a car is not a car
in a showroom, polished and still.

My idea of galactic travel
is a road through space.

My idea of color is evergreens
against a blue sky, snow below.

My idea of ideas is vague,
conceptual, fragmented, fluid.

My idea of the unknowable
is something I know too well.

My idea of a night on the town
is staying home in the country.

My idea of a basket is your lap.
My idea was to steal your ideas

until I became you.

What I Might Have Done

Sleek starlings flying low
    over whitecaps on the bay
        remind me of Ortygia,

so far from where I am,
    exactly where I wish
        to stroll the white stones

of Piazza Duomo,
    stop in at the bookstore
        for tea and conversation,

buy tuna at the market,
    a bottle of Nero d'Avola
        to sip while fish grills

just outside my flat,
    no radio stations to ruin
        my slow course of thought,

no trains to disturb my reverie,
    no looking back at what
        I might have done differently.

II

How Silent the Trees

— in memory of Liam Rector

How the hell are you, I want
to ask but can't—you're dead.

How hard the snow fell,
how slowly it melts.

How to tie a knot big enough
to choke the wild pain.

How to listen carelessly
to words used carefully.

How answers to questions
often contain no answer.

How to wind a watch
so tight time stops.

How silent the trees, how
loud the shots of hunters.

Hurricane

We lie in its eye,
watch birds strain
to fly straight

into a funnel
that spins them
inward, their wings

thrust sideways,
feathers a carpet
we grip as it twists,

as it lifts us off
this earth we bet
would never raise us,

gravity a collar
we were sure
would keep us down.

Pity

No quarter is given to humiliation,
self-immolation, here in a state
of impure Puritan congratulation.

Watch the river flow in two directions,
one that leads to the sea, one to me,
where I wade, and wait, thirsty.

Quake

Seismic disturbances
disturb us, size us
up for future reactions
to movements of earth.
Inhalations of breath
mean life is still here,
dodgy as it is on Mars,
where we belong, red
dirt cowboys on fire,
liars who never leave home
for store or space station,
impatient to carry on
with our sci-fi lives,
the hives of bees we keep
for times like these, buzzing
like those who caused them.

Pulse

I put my hand on your wrist
not just to feel your skin
but to feel the blood that races
from heart to fingertip
and back, another lap
of the city of you.

Pulse of the city, pulse
of your state, pulse
of the nation contained
in your veins, vines
that grow grapes whose
wine we press tonight:
licorice, mineral, spirit.

Drummer

A bass drum's beat
wakes her in the night.
She goes to the window,
looks out and sees nothing,
but the pounding continues.

It's her heart she hears
above the noise of fans,
crickets, the refrigerator
that keeps her wine cold
as the night she met him.

He didn't look like a drummer
or act like one, no hands
beating time on the table
in the tiny dark bar
he took her to twice.

Time waits for no one,
he said, and she thought
Stones but didn't say it,
just played it straight
as he sang her praises.

He never called back,
just sent a postcard
that said *Still drumming.*

Sort it Out

Sort who or what
is not shot from
who or what
is in fact shot

Sort them by
torment
the heart
a soft target

Predict when
this may
or may not
happen again

Sort storm clouds
from war clouds
from clouds
we live under

Mixup at the Speakeasy

She says she is on again,
off again, as if opposites
explain her to us, which they do.

Through her window she watched the towers
come down, her eyes darker now.
Her hair lies flat on her head.

The wind blew her into our doorway
which we opened to her story.
The wind has ceased but she has not.

No detail of her life is too small
or personal, no building or tale too tall.
We can't wait to turn her off again.

Her Measured Fall

Deterred at first
      her byway cursed
           she dropped her guard

Her measured fall
      too small to feel
           to hear or touch

Quiet darling
      sirens singing
           ashes ashes

                all fall down

Gravity

Out of night-blooming jasmine,
      out of queen of the night
            come rays of light that slice
      darkness, drive us toward
jagged, unfair ground

from which we push
      up and out, against gravity
            we abhor, that wants us
      to adore it, force that pulls
against our ache.

Owls perch in jasmine
      vines, scan for lunch,
            screech vowels across
                  canyons of sound,
            twist their necks so far
      it hurts to watch, to snatch
snippets of consonant shriek.

Sound pulls us down against our will,
      brash sirens, jackhammers acking
            all the live-long day. Away

                from this I want to go. Away.

Counting

My tires grip a narrow lane
of dirt in wet-green woods
where sheep cross before me.

Just sheared, they will not
look my way, their bleats
an awkward symphony of loss.

I think of soldiers limping home,
their eyes on the road I missed,
gravel grinding under their boots.

I count them.

The Loneliest Road in America

— in memory of Kurt Brown

Dusk is the hour   between dog and wolf
howling and howling   where is my darling

why this highway   endless and stark
a zigzag line   across Nevada

mirages rise   over vanishing points
out of focus   out of mind

when the sun   drops from sight
le rayon vert   flares once and dissolves

my car glides west   escorted by stars
miles of pavement   listening hard

my ears can't block   the wails of coyotes
when I run out of gas   far from a town

I find a red shirt   to wave for help
there are no cars   I need no help

I wave instead   at epitaphs
I find on stones   beside the highway

III

Collected Works

A brown cardboard box
packed tight with books
no one troubled to read

drifts over our heads
buoyed on the heat
of its own invention.

Needles and Haste

One, two, I count on you
     to remember your password,
         how to spell your name,

the past composed
     of black and white photos
         you never developed

of ghosts from a closet
     you don't open for fear
         of what you'll expose.

Nine, ten, the numbers
     you give the doctor
         for the pain you're in,

the routes you drove in on,
     the way you give nothing
         else up to him, standing

in his white jacket,
     hand on hip, in a room
         of needles and haste.

Vectors

The hole in my head's getting bigger,
expanding at the pace of my heart
which pumps hard to help me
survive vectors of toxins aimed
my way. Blood is everywhere,
not just mine but everyone's, nuns
in France, sheiks in Bahrain, running
down drains in shower floors,
spilling down stairways in waves,
through gates no one thought to close.

Gunfire

Gunfire in the night wakes me
in bed: I cower under covers.
The last shot comes through the wall
just under your photo, framed
in gilt, your smile disarming,
flight in your eyes. The bullet
hole lets winter air blow in,
chill I know well.

At dawn the hunters return
to gather their kill, drag it
slowly back to their truck
in my driveway, speed away
with Skynyrd at volume,
name of their state on their
license plate, numbers that add up
to sixteen, number of days
since you went away.

Intense

Intense is an
intriguing word:
could mean strong,
severe, extreme; could
mean in actual tents,
could mean homicides
gone terribly
awry, getaway
cars out of fuel,
the pale drivers
slumped over their
steering wheels, dead
from exhaust fumes.

We live in a tent
and it's intense,
the winter colder
than falling snow
which covers our tent
and warms it until
it caves in on us,
the last straw,
the silver dollar
no one wants,
the albino deer
dead on the trail.

Death of the Cool

Breath on a spool
that unwinds into
sounds so loud
they injure ears,
find fear in chords
so rare they haven't
been invented yet,
make stops where
others would keep
playing, scatter eerie
notes across a room
that stands in
for everywhere
else.

The trumpet glistens
in the low bar
light, sends furtive
signals to the bass
and drums, a guitar
that sounds like
gutters might
if they were tuned
to a station
devoted to loss,
sounds so severe
no one seems able
to make them
stop.

Tread Lightly

Tread lightly on the water, or sink.
Go into your room and don't come out.
Trip on a word you're trying to learn.
Don't stop talking, even to yourself.
Lower your voice—it echoes in here.
Try every coat on, buy or steal none.
Get in your car without knowing why.
Time the stoplights so you get every red.
Tip the waitress more than necessary.
Train your eyes on everything around you.
Look in the mirror, see someone else.

Harvest Moon

Harvest moon rises as I fall
from grace, two stories down
from the roof I built of pine
and oak, pining for you now
as I lie on the ground looking up
at birds I mistake for planes.

They fly straight south in V
formation, no information
on where you went or when you might
return to save my broken body.
I hear their calls from here below,
try to compose an imitation.

Trapped in a Decade Long Gone

Freedom's like a beehive,
take too much and you're stung,
punished for your needs,
banished from your local.

Loss isn't fleeting:
it's physical, durable
as a car battery
until the day it dies.

Sounds in my head contain
tambourine men, echoes
of masters, ruinous
sledge hammers. Then silence.

Sometimes similes go astray,
strut down avenues of glory
unaware of their uselessness,
trapped in a decade long gone.

She Erased His Mouth

Soliloquy of eleven words,
What the hell are you doing?
Fantasia Fest in Provincetown,
Who is that you're kissing?

But you kissed her too,
in the bar's ladies' room,
and had to admit
she had nice lips.

Her husband a bigot,
his mouth a spigot
no one could turn off
until we silenced him.

Silence for her was
kissing someone else,
tongues too entwined
to say anything.

Desperation
clouded her almond eyes
until, kissing others,
she erased his face.

We knew she wanted
to erase the rest of him
but kissed us instead—
in a bar, not a bed.

Alaska

When she speaks at length of job creation
        under the current administration, I'm
too busy changing her oil to understand.

When he tells me he's going into seclusion
        I pack him a box of power bars and books
to help sustain his hefty illusion.

When they tell me they're seeing each other
        I call Alaska and rent a cabin.
Then I call both their mothers.

When I get to Alaska it's cold as hell:
        No one bothered to tell me this.
I cover my body with oil from whales.

No one calls me—there's no phone.
        I know how to get the hard jobs done.
Then I learn to like to be alone.

Pirated

Rapscallions in the galley
    overcome me with their smell
        on a galleon with three masts
    bent to the task of sailing straight
into a brutal east wind.

I tremble at their immense odor,
    thrown starboard to port and back.
        I shudder like the sails,
    head a riddle, stomach muddled,
the sea heaving below us all.

I sail these perilous waters
    because I can't stand land.
        No matter the hazard I go,
    sometimes aboard schooners
less than savory, but I go.

I met a man in the Azores
    who swore he could make me
        a pirate, would give
    me swagger if I'd sniff
what he had on his dagger

which put me in a stupor,
    a nightmare that began
        and ended with pirates,
    models for the bad guy
I was but am not now.

That storm has passed.

Debris

we pause to observe

what is submerged

float over debris

that looks like ours

wait to see

what we can keep

IV

Abstraction

The abstraction of Rothko
square clouds on canvas

The drips of Pollock
rain that pours down

Snow squall lip balm
hands in our pockets

The dream of spring
still just a dream

Dust swirls in our eyes
motes from the past

Flames singe skin
no math explains that

The sadness of computers
the looks on cows' faces

Vespers vespers vespers
the quietude of hours

Trees blow sideways
sun gone for the season

Table set for two
the aroma of garlic

Coyote crying in the night
stars that never end

Drinking the Stars

Petite bubbles rise
in the wine beneath
his nose, before
his eyes, eyes
not used to such
a thing, brain
not trained to
understand
liquid alchemy.

A fresh elixir
enters his mouth
in the cool cellar
of the monastery
without bidding
or prayer, layers
of lush lemon,
carnal almond,
weightless and dense
at once, enough
finish to finish
even a monk
off.

Menu

She dances through the kitchen door,
grins twice as she recites
tonight's menu: paté on lavash,
leg of lamb, Amarone.

Her nose says all is not right
out in the speeded-up world,
but close to her stove the smell
is slow, Mediterranean.

Friends go on with petty fights
but she alights on a stool,
stirs three sauces on this day
her daily bread, leavened or not
here she comes, tongue on fire
with flavor, her body floating on air.

Parade

Here in the postcoital economy
no one can afford a cigarette,
much less a light to help find
the way to bathroom or bar,
cloakroom or car that waits
in the garage for gasoline
so dear it's only a dream,
like the one of recovery,
financial or otherwise,
a hypothesis proved
by the graph below,
so slow to move
upward or
across.

                                     Here
                                 in our bed
                            there's light
                       at the far end of
                    the tunnel of love,
               and a tiny British car
            we only dream of driving
          over the cliff we call wedlock
        but opt instead for hairpin turns
      which throw our bodies together
    as if for the first time, in this same
  red roadster as many long years ago
as there are lines in this stanza, which
float down the page like us in a parade.

Three Loves

I gave three loves away:
one to books, one to hooks,
and one love to you,
which you kept close.

I gave three loaves away
in California:
one to Alice, a poet,
one to Gregg, a lawyer,
one to a homeless girl
on Telegraph Avenue.

I gave three lives away:
one to work, one to play,
one to what I saw
when I closed my eyes.

Flow

The guy working on the ceiling lights
in Penney's reaches up so far
I can read the tattoo
just above his belt,
I LOVE FLOW,
which reminds me of my neighbors
who drilled wells for a living
and were from the 60s,
and as a result of one
or both of these facts
painted GO WITH THE FLOW
in blue cursive letters
on their red barn,
the four words I saw
on those days when I looked up
from my awful brown shoes
and planned to follow
their sage advice
and knew that I would not.

Belief

Be careful what you believe:
Men on the moon, gravity.
Leaves that change color,
fall far from grace.

Believe in blues outtakes,
stones that skip on ponds.
Kites that twist in the wind,
shake loose from strings, drift
down to those who wait.

The Watcher

A long house on a long hill
      in the middle distance, close enough
to see a woman pace back and forth
      as if in deep thought or suspense.

When she stops and turns my way
      does she see me or someone else
she knew remotely, before
      she lived like this, on the hill?

The woods reel me in, pull me
      away from her silhouette there, '
so thin, nose almost aquiline,
      hair orange as a car on fire.

Bushes and weeds overtake me,
      push me back into hard ground.

Documents

Documents stir in the breeze
but do not leave the desk.

They may be letters never
delivered, emotions
composed in distress
to X, missives meant
to calm the addressee,

returned to the sender
who expired before learning
X never found her way
across the Aegean,

words that need wind
to sail them out the window
through exhausted air
into an overgrown field
where a dumpster sits,

as full of ink as it can get,
as empty as we let it be.

Film

Two rhythms: a conga, a snare

Pan from green hills
to couple strolling
a textbook English lawn

she lengthens her gait
to try to match his

insert dialogue here

Beyond them a meadow
where horses nip tulips
behind a stone house

Soften percussion
slow beat of a quiet heart

Afternoon becomes evening
tea at three too weak
thus the return to dialogue

which goes here

Closeup of couple debating
she almost takes his point

her face is pinched
he doesn't notice
his face in his hands

The lamp behind them burns

Starboard

Wind rips hard
from starboard

my boat lacks sails

lacks stars   to steer me
east northeast

where you   my heart

still drift

The Road Ends Here

Due to the nature of my absence
I will write with more frequency.
In the middle of my life I've gone
to find a drive-in that shows movies
from the past, loops of film I love.
It's warm and I can sleep
in my car, drive away if asked.

ACKNOWLEDGMENTS

Academy of American Poets Poem-a-Day (online): "Mars Poetica"
AGNI (online): "How Silent the Trees," "My Idea"
Blackbird (online): "Abstraction," "Menu," "Vectors"
Bluestem: "Gravity," "Harvest Moon"
City Art Journal: "Mixup at the Speakeasy"
Crab Creek Review: "Flow," "This Train"
Diode Poetry Journal (online): "Drinking the Stars," "Sort it Out"
Ducts (online): "Pulse," "Quake"
Five Points: "Lifeboat," "Plaza de Toros"
Gihon River Review: "The Kind of Rain"
Green Mountains Review: "Angels," "Needles and Haste,"
        "Three Loves," "Trapped in a Decade Long Gone"
Hollins Critic: "Collected Works," "The Road Ends Here"
KA Confidential: "Viral"
Map Literary (online): "Death of the Cool," "Tread Lightly"
Salamander: "This Lightness," "What I Might Have Done"
The Salon: "Pity"
Slate (online): "Movement"
Slope (online): "Film"
Sugar House Review: "Alaska," "Parade"
Terminus: "Gunfire," "Intense," "The Loneliest Road
        in America"
Vermont Magazine: "The Watcher"
Western Humanities Review: "Rosemary's Babies"

"Plaza de Toros" also appeared on the *Poetry Daily* website.

THANK YOU

To the editors who published some of these poems, Robert Pinsky, Elizabeth Powell, Katharine Coles, Sven Birkerts, Hanna Andrews, Valerie Duff, Jennifer Barber, Megan Sexton, Josh Russell, Charlotte Pence, Amy Lemmon, Travis Denton, Cindy Whitman, Martha Silano, Greg Donovan, Mary Flinn, Cathy Hankla, Nano Taggart, and Christopher Salerno.

For honest and perceptive readings of the manuscript, Katharine Coles, Valerie Duff, Shawna Parker, and Dennis Maloney.

For close readings of individual poems, Ralph Wilson, Marty Williams, Charlotte Pence, Chris Merrill, Andrea Rogers, Kevin McLellan, Ralph Pennel, Ron Spalletta, Curtis Perdue, and Richard Burns.

And for welcoming me back home, Dennis Maloney and Elaine LaMattina.

Wyn Cooper has published four previous books of poetry, most recently *Chaos is the New Calm* (BOA Editions, 2010). His poems, stories, essays, and reviews have appeared in *Poetry, Ploughshares, AGNI, The Southern Review, Five Points, Slate,* and more than 100 other magazines. His poems are included in twenty-five anthologies of contemporary poetry, including *Poetry: An Introduction, The Mercury Reader, Outsiders,* and *Ecstatic Occasions, Expedient Forms.*

In 1993, "Fun," a poem from his first book, was turned into Sheryl Crow's Grammy-winning song "All I Wanna Do." He has also cowritten songs with David Broza, David Baerwald, Jody Redhage, and Bill Bottrell. In 2003, Gaff Music released *Forty Words for Fear,* an album of songs based on poems and lyrics by Cooper, set to music and sung by the novelist Madison Smartt Bell. Their second album, *Postcards Out of the Blue,* based in part on Cooper's postcard poems, was released in 2008. Their songs have been featured on six television shows.

Cooper has taught at the University of Utah, Bennington College, Marlboro College, and at The Frost Place. He has given readings across the country, as well as in Europe. He is a former editor of *Quarterly West,* and the recipient of a fellowship from the Ucross Foundation. For two years he worked at the Harriet Monroe Poetry Institute, a think tank run by the Poetry Foundation. He lives in Boston and works as a freelance editor.

www.wyncooper.com